1,111 Excuses, Evasions, White Lies and Fibs

Candice Canny / Fine Findig

1,111 Excuses, Evasions, White Lies and Fibs

For being late or not coming at all,
for things not done and mishaps,
for speeding and parking,
for bad grades, bad karma,
and other human weaknesses ...

Bibliografische Information der Deutschen
Nationalbibliothek: Die Deutsche Nationalbibliothek
verzeichnet diese Publikation in der Deutschen
Nationalbibliografie; detaillierte bibliografische
Daten sind im Internet über http://dnb.dnb.de
abrufbar.
Bibliographic information of the German National
Library: The German National Library lists this
publication in the German National Bibliography;
detailed bibliographic data are available on the
Internet at http://dnb.dnb.de.

© 2022 the author behind Fine Findig/Candice Canny
Herstellung und Verlag: BoD – Books on Demand,
Norderstedt, Germany
ISBN: 9783755756798

Content

Excuses For The Brave... 113

Preliminary remarks

Being late or forgetting an appointment, not completing a task, getting a bad grade at school or being unavailable–time and again in life there are unpleasant situations in which you need a good explanation for omissions and misfortunes.

It's not longer hard to know what to do, because among the 1,111 excuses, evasions, white lies and fibs, you're sure to find one that gives you a good explanation.

The explanations are not all to be taken seriously. Some excuses are quite humorous, others are cheeky and provocative, and finally there are some quite fantastic ones.

One more important note: Whether you use the excuse for parking illegally or for not paying bills, there is of course no guarantee and no warranty that you will get away with it. This depends, among other things, on how well and credibly you can present your excuse.

Good luck–and above all, have fun!

Coming too late or not at all: Excuses for all occasions

Only minutes or even hours: You are late

Ever since my alarm clock fell off last week, it hasn't worked properly.

The lock on the front door wouldn't open from the inside, so I had to call a locksmith to even get out.

My grandma had misplaced her third teeth and I had to help look for them.

I overtook a lorry and missed the exit. Then I had to drive the whole distance to the next exit. *(It looks even more credible if you give more precise details about the exit and the extra kilometres/miles).*

I thought it was Saturday. It wasn't until I got the newspaper that I realised it was only Friday.

The motorway was so full that even the exits were jammed.

There were problems with the species-appropriate accommodation of Franzi. *(When asked who Franzi is, come up with an answer like my tortoise, my budgie, my wife or similar).*

The pedestrian lights didn't turn green and I didn't want to set a bad example for the children next to me.

The electric gate of my garage didn't open this morning.

The deodorant I put on this morning made me faint.

Do you know Murphy's Law? Well, you see: I couldn't come on time at all. *(Murphy's Law or Murphy's Law says nothing else than: If something can go wrong, it will certainly go wrong).*

The queue at the metro exit was so big that it just took so long to get out of there.

I thought the discounter was selling PCs mega-cheap again, so I stood in line for over an hour. But either there were none or they were already sold out, in any case I didn't get one.

God didn't wake me up today. She's usually so reliable.

I couldn't leave the house, my wife had taken all the trousers to the cleaners.

Time had stopped. Or so I thought and waited for the end of the world. It was only hours later that I realised it was only the clock that had stopped.

I had to go past the bank this morning and the bank card got stuck– I had to pop it out again with pliers. *(You might even be able to fray an old card on the side a bit and show it off).*

At breakfast, a filling fell out and I had to go to the dentist urgently.

I had accidentally taken an overdose of the cough medicine this morning– suddenly I felt dizzy and had to lie down.

The tram had a power cut.

I couldn't find the book with the excuses. A friend of mine needed it badly.

There was a politician's car on the road and everything was jammed behind the motorcade of important people and policemen.

The central locking from the car would not open.

I took my parents to the train today and carried the suitcase into the compartment. The train left while I was still on it. I got off at the next station and am now waiting for a return ticket.

I got on the train in the wrong direction. *(Works for buses and trams too, of course).*

13

I had the tax investigation in the house and had to quickly hide my black money.

I'm on a diet at the moment and it's upset my internal clock.

The narrow tyres of my bike got caught in the tram tracks, even though the train was already running, and because of the traffic behind me I couldn't just stop, but had to get to the stop at the station. Only there could I stop, turn around and ride back safely on the tarmac.

I broke down, got my trousers dirty and went home to change.

I had forgotten that it was my wedding day and had to stop at the flower shop.

There's a bull terrier sitting outside my front door and every time I open the door he wants to attack me. I wait a while, maybe he'll go away on his own, I'll come later.

A lorry broke down and there was no way to overtake it and I couldn't turn around either.

Tonight I met xxx *(insert name of celebrity here)* and the dream was so good that I didn't wake up until 9 o'clock *(or 10 o'clock or even later)*.

I need to have the navigation system in the car checked—the thing completely misled me.

To be perfectly honest: I was still too drunk to drive to work this morning. Responsible as I am, I therefore decided to stay at home.

The city is one big construction site and I didn't understand the traffic routing with the one-way streets. I drove in circles for half an hour.

The barriers from the level crossing just wouldn't go up, even though the train had passed a long time ago.

The fire brigade had closed the road because there was a smell of gas in the air.

Obviously, I misunderstood the instructions for my new alarm clock.

My son/little brother fell off his bike and broke his leg, I had to make sure he got medical attention first.

The dry cleaners opened later today, so I didn't get to my suit in time.

The neighbour's cat was high up in the tree and couldn't get down–and my ladder was the only one long enough to get there.

I wanted to call and say that I would be late, but I had no network, there must have been a dead zone.

There was a dog abandoned by the road and I didn't find my way to the shelter right away.

My daughter/my ex-wife/whoever had a fresh pimple and was suicidal.

My tyre was flat and since I'm not very skilled at changing tyres, it took a little longer.

My wife must have brought the wrong clothes from the dry cleaners, the trousers were far too small.

An excavator broke down in front of my driveway—it was impossible to get past it.

The tram switch was wrong and by the time we got to the transfer stop, the connecting tram had gone.

When I wanted to get out of the garage, construction workers had dug up the road and I had to wait until the ditch was covered with a slab.

This morning every, but really every traffic light was on red.

15

A friend called me and started crying because her boyfriend had left her. Whenever I wanted to end the conversation, she hinted at suicidal tendencies, so I was stuck on the phone for hours until she calmed down to some extent.

I thought I had a radio-controlled clock that changed to daylight saving time by itself. *(Only fits if you're an hour late just after the time change in spring).*

I accidentally drank decaffeinated coffee and fell asleep at the breakfast table.

My little sister had an exam this morning and was so panicked that I had to talk her into it first.

The neighbour's rooster didn't crow this morning. Maybe he's already in the cooking pot. I don't know how I'll wake up tomorrow.

A concrete mixer tipped over in the bend in front of the house and all the concrete was lying around on the road.

I was late because I spent so long looking for a matching pair of socks. Since we started using the new detergent, I can only find single socks–the others seem to be dissolved by the suds ...

A huge branch from the old tree crashed into the road tonight and the fire brigade's chainsaw was broken. Everyone in the neighbourhood sawed it apart by hand.

Water pipe burst in the flat opposite. And because the neighbour is so scatterbrained, I took care of it myself. Otherwise it might have run under my door.

Because of a power cut last night, the time on the clock radio was wrong.

I had accidentally set the clock to the wrong time zone.

Due to climate change, a tree died and fell across the road. It was not possible to drive around the tree and there were lots of other cars jammed up behind me.

Some jokers put liquid glue in the door lock of the car. I can't get the door open.

Totally overslept, my cat must have knocked the alarm clock off the bedside table last night, it was lying on the floor this morning.

All the cars were snowed in, I shovelled and shovelled, but unfortunately shovelled the wrong car free. And then I walked around puzzling over which pile of snow my car was under. *(Of course, this only works in a snowy winter!)*.

My car didn't start, so I hitchhiked, but the tractor I was riding on was a bit slow.

My grandmother was standing on the balcony and couldn't open the door to the flat, so I climbed over the neighbouring flat to her to push open the jammed door. That cost me some time.

An old man fell down in front of me and I took him to the doctor. But thank God nothing was broken.

I'll be late today. Spent the night at my friend's and poured coffee over my fresh clothes, now I have to go home first to change.

I couldn't find my contact lens and I can't drive a car without it.

My son/little brother has double and triple knotted the laces on all his shoes. It took me a lot of time to unknot at least one pair of shoes.

There must be a marten in our neighbourhood that eats the cables. Tonight it was my car.

I wasn't in the mental condition to endure the crowdedness on public transport this morning, so I walked–it just takes longer.

The bus driver overlooked me at the bus stop and drove past.

Just as I was about to leave, a hoover salesman arrived and refused to be turned away.

I've been feeling so sick in the mornings for the last few days that I've been sitting on the toilet for hours until I finally feel better.

There was tree cutting work on the neighbour's property and one of the tree cutters didn't estimate the direction of the fall correctly. Now the tree is blocking my front door, I can't get out.

But you said the other day that I should have a nice evening. Now I've had a nice evening and you don't like it.

Sorry, but a door was stuck on the children's advent calendar.

On the bus I saw the man of my life and just followed him— unfortunately he picked up his wife somewhere.

I had to finish reading the crime novel and unmask the murderer first–the suspense would have killed me today otherwise.

(Groan.) Invited to mother-in-law's for dinner last night. *(Groan.)* Miserable cook, always knew. But it's never been this bad before. Maybe it was the fish.

The hairdresser's visit yesterday was a complete failure, I had to be restored first thing this morning, before that I couldn't get on the road.

The hamster escaped from the cage and bit the cable from the clock radio.

The spark plug connector on my moped/scooter was loose and I hadn't noticed.

Laxative in the cocktail last night, a joke from my friends–I was stuck all morning.

At confession this morning I was saddled with 27 Our Fathers, just finished.

I was in a traffic jam, took a turn and then got completely lost.

My dog had flatulence and these farts were so stinky that I fainted after the third fart and only came to after hours. But now my dog is fine again, thank God.

That relationship drama on TV last night depressed me so much that I had to motivate myself for a very long time this morning.

My washing machine leaked this morning, it took ages to get the whole floor dry again.

I had to go to the bank urgently and then it took me hours to decode the secret code I had carefully encrypted.

The car's on-board computer said that there was enough petrol for 50 kilometer/miles–but I still broke down because I ran out of petrol.

The elderly woman living upstairs fell down the stairs and I took care of her until the ambulance arrived.

The TV programme yesterday was so boring that I fell asleep in the living room, where I don't have an alarm clock.

Plagued by nightmares, I only fell into a deep sleep this morning. But now I'm here–fresh and alert.

19

I'm fostering my aunt's dog and it escaped from me while I was walking it today. It was quite an operation to catch him again. But without the dog I would have died.

I think the driver of the rubbish truck was drunk this morning. He threw all the rubbish bins on the road with the truck, there was no way through the chaos.

I broke off the car key on the driver's side and then called the garage. It took an hour for them to come. And then another hour to change the lock.

The electrical system of the windscreen wipers is broken, so I had to go through the car wash to get a clear view.

Ran into a bike check and because my light was faulty, I had to walk the rest of the way.

I'm late? Then my mother/wife entered the wrong time in the calendar.

Obviously the alarm clock rang while I was on the toilet. Since I didn't hear the ringing, I went back to bed and fell deeply asleep again.

My alarm clock rings less and less often. I wonder if it's because it's a cheap Asian product.

(In a higher building:) I had a terrible nightmare today with falling lifts, so I took the stairs. You wouldn't believe how long it takes.

Sorry, but I couldn't find a parking space!

When I looked out of the window, the chimney sweep was falling from the roof next door. So I had to call an ambulance first.

There was a diversion sign that I followed and at some point I came out somewhere else. If the friendly taxi driver hadn't shown me the way, I would still be on my way here.

I was in a bear costume for a children's birthday party last night and didn't come out all night. My friend tried to cut the costume with scissors this morning and stabbed her foot. I have to go to the doctor now.

The instructions for my new alarm clock are so complicated that I didn't manage to programme it properly last night.

Last night I dreamt of the last tie game of Manchester. And then the game went into overtime.

I got into a vehicle inspection and had to clear out the whole boot to be able to show the first-aid kit and warning triangle.

Something's wrong with my watch, it ran faster than I did today.

I was already at the bus stop when I remembered that I hadn't turned off the coffee machine.

The bus driver was new on the route and got completely lost. Just don't buy any retreads! I had one burst this morning. It cost me a lot of time and nerves.

My car key fell down the drain.

Our mother-in-law is visiting us and she blocked the bathroom for two hours this morning.

Had to fill up quickly and fainted because of the price of the petrol ...

Do you know this? You're driving on a narrow country road and there's a tractor in front of you that takes up the whole width of the road? You see, that's why it took me half an hour to get to the motorway today.

It's bad how dependent you've already become on these computers. This morning my navigation system failed and I promptly got lost.

21

I don't understand it, I ran out of petrol and the fuel gauge was still before the last line.

The heating meter reader said he'd come at half past nine, but he didn't show up until half past nine.

I had an appointment with my accountant and fainted there for a long time over back taxes.

My grandpa is getting more and more forget-ful. Last night he called because the heart medicine was all, and because he needs it urgently, I had to go to the pharmacy first thing this morning.

The idiot in front of me stopped one metre before the contact loop. That's why the traffic light didn't change to green. And when I tried to explain this to him, he started another argument with me.

I asked for directions and was sent completely astray.

I pulled the short match tomorrow and had to wait for the others to finish in the bathroom.

I'm sorry, but I got off the bus five stops earlier because I was squeezed in next to someone who was intolerable to my olfactory receptors. Nearly fainted.

The stock market in Paramaribo has crashed, my fortune is gone and I'm going to see my psychiatrist now. *(Hard to check: Paramaribo is in Suriname, a stock market crash there will hardly appear in the media here).*

I completely lost my orientation in the thick fog.

Something is wrong with my heart rhythm. I went to the clinic this morning to have the pacemaker checked.

I was in such a hurry that I got flashed–and then sorting out the formalities caused me the delay.

The dog ate the car key. Now we have to hitchhike to the vet. The operation will take a little longer.

Well, I burnt my breakfast bacon in the pan, and when my neighbour saw how much smoke was coming out of the window, he thought everything was on fire and stupidly called the fire brigade. You wouldn't believe what they did to my kitchen...

The key to the wardrobe broke off and I didn't want to come to the office naked either. So I had to pick the lock first.

For some reaon a farmer drove his flock of thousands of sheep through town. All the roads were blocked by sheep gawking stupidly.

My doctor said I needed to walk more. So I didn't come by car this morning, but on foot.

My daughter left with my car last night and hasn't been back yet this morning.

My dog got hypo-glycaemia, lay there completely apathetic, I immediately had to go to the vet.

I'm afraid I read the city map upside down. All of a sudden, north and south were reversed.

I pressed too hard on the toothpaste tube this morning and it took me ages to get the too much toothpaste back into the tube.

It might happen: You don't come at all

Actually, I only have a harmless flu, but I don't think I can tolerate the medicine I took. Now I have a headache, dizziness, stomach ache, and everything else that's on the package insert.

23

Every time I wanted to go out, the radio announcer told me to stay on the line.

Did you read about this terrible misfortune in the newspaper? My parents/my sisters/etc. were among the victims, so surely you understand that I couldn't/can't come.

My radio clock hasn't received a signal for days, I have no sense of time at all. Is it Wednesday now?

I'm superstitious, and there was a ladder outside the front door that I would have had to walk under. I couldn't leave the house then.

There was a raid in our neighbourhood, the police were looking for drug lords and arrested me. It was only in the evening that they admitted they had made a mistake and let me go. My lawyer will give them a run for their money now, I can tell you that.

I can't come to work today, there's a score to settle with my last boss who fired me for not coming to work.

I had to shovel snow this morning and lost the key to the front door and the car, so I spent the whole day digging through the snow pile for the key. *(Only works in winter when it snows, of course).*

Tonight, a young bull broke out of a stable on a farm and went on a rampage through the neighbourhood. The police shot him dead in front of my garage, of all places, and it will take a while before the report is written and the carcass is taken away.

I was about to leave when a wasp stung me and I have an allergic reaction to that. *(Watch out: Wasps, bees and the like don't fly when it's cold, only from about 10 degrees).*

My aunt died and as she had no children, I now have to take care of all the formalities.

I have an insane headache and can't come. Maybe it will be better by tomorrow or the day after.

My cat had kittens tonight and I've been tying umbilical cords all night.

Since last night I have been suffering from trigeminal neuralgia. With rest and darkness, I hope to get it under control in a day or two. *(Inflammation of the facial nerve with severe pain attacks).*

My very pregnant neighbour went into labour and I took her to hospital. There the doctor mistook me for the father and forced me to stay the whole time. It turned out to be a pretty girl.

I'm suffering a bout of agoraphobia at the moment and can't leave the house today. *(Agoraphobia: the fear of space, i.e. open streets and places).*

I feel sick, I think it's because of the sushi dinner last night.

A pride of lions escaped from the zoo and the whole street was blocked off. They also cut the telephone lines so that the press wouldn't find out and the population wouldn't panic. These are the conditions in this country ...

Of course it sounds unbelievable, but I drove out into the countryside last night, then my car broke down in a forest, my mobile phone had no network connection, I then ran off, had to spend the night in the forest, lost my wallet in the dark and then needed the whole day to hitchhike home.

The neighbour had to go to the doctor urgently and I looked after the children. Unfortunately, the case was more complicated and she only came back in the afternoon. You wouldn't believe what a relief that was, because my hearing was suffering a lot from the children's screaming.

I fell out of bed so violently from the ringing of the alarm clock that I lay there unconscious all day.

Climate change and the fate of polar bears in the Arctic made me so desperate to get out of the house this morning. I can't come today, my husband is sleepwalking and when I wake up this morning he is not in the house. I wonder where he ran off to tonight. Before yesterday it was only the garage.

My wife needed the car, she's gone back to her mother's.

(At 9 o'clock:) I overslept, but I'm on my way now. *(At 12 o'clock:)* I don't understand, I fell asleep again dressed at the breakfast table, I'm coming now. *(The next day:)* Unbelievable, but I fell asleep again, I think I'm sick, go to the doctor.

Whenever I have so much stress, I get oesophagitis, and now it's happening again. *(Oesophagitis is an inflammation of the oesophagus, symptoms are heartburn and belching).*

Fell asleep again watching breakfast TV and didn't wake up until the evening news.

I accidentally changed the time from the Gregorian to the Julian calendar. *(According to the Julian calendar, a year has 365.25 days; according to the Gregorian, only 365.2425. Since the introduction of the Gregorian calendar, the Julian calendar is now about two weeks behind).*

26

What do I know what's flying today: Birch, hazelnut or house dust. Anyway, his eyes and nose are completely swollen shut. I hope it will be better tomorrow.

I slipped in the shower and twisted my ankle. I can't even manage to put my shoes on.

My neighbour was once again so beaten up by her husband that I had to spend the whole day putting her up at the women's shelter, dealing with the Youth Welfare Office and then dealing with the divorce lawyer for her. The poor woman is completely helpless on her own.

My uncle is arriving at the airport today, and since he only has one arm but two suitcases, I have to pick him up.

The house next door is a construction site right now and some stupid truck driver dumped all the gravel on my driveway.

I was invited to dinner last night and foolishly opted for the mushroom stew. This morning, unfortunately, my nervous system is still a bit scratched. One of the mushrooms must have been a bit poisonous.

There's no way I'm coming today. Last night I tried a new hair colour, now I have squeaky pink hair and I'm going to the hairdresser first, maybe he can still save something, otherwise I'll have to shave it off.

My new girlfriend's ex is so jealous that he nailed my front door shut last night so I can't see her. Unfortunately, I can't go to work today either, I have to call the handyman first.

My bull terrier got nipped by a small dachshund yesterday, now he's so depressed I have to take him to the therapist.

My love horoscope predicts many erotic hours today–honestly, what am I doing in the office?

I was followed by a black limousine on my way to your place–I had to lose it first.

My little sister locked me in the bathroom and couldn't figure out how to get the door open again. Of course, I didn't have the phone with me to call for help. *(Of course, you can also do that with your little daughter, your little nephew or another little child).*

When my lottery numbers were drawn, I just had to go celebrate. But you don't have to worry: when I was paying, I found the lottery ticket in my wallet—imagine, I hadn't even handed it in!

What? It's already Wednesday? Then I've slept 32 hours straight! From Monday until this morning! Crazy!

I passed a church on the way and an inner voice advised me to talk to God–and you know how elderly and lonely people like to talk and talk and talk, I couldn't get away.

My eyes were so swollen shut this morning that I couldn't even find my shoes. That's not normal! I think I should go for an allergy test.

I had stupidly walled myself in during the remodelling of the house and my wife only noticed where I was after two days.

I have to extend my weekend holiday, my plane ticket and all my papers have been stolen, I'm not getting out of here any time soon.

There must be someone else in town with my name. Anyway, I was innocently arrested and by the time my lawyer had sorted it out, the day was over.

The whole world talks about self-discovery, and when I'm looking for myself, you want to take away a day's holiday right away?

My doctor discovered a new disease in me. It's so new that it's not even in the medical dictionary. Now he wants to continue intensive testing over the next few days.

I was tending the neighbours' dog and when I went to put food in the doghouse, I got stuck in the narrow opening. It was only in the evening that the other neighbour heard my cries for help.

Yesterday evening I hooked up my new e-car to the charging station and this morning found that the battery is still empty. Until the battery has halfway charged, the day is over.

I've been afraid of crowds since the weekend. I'm not coming in today until everyone's off work. My children put glue on the toilet seat and thought it was terribly funny. At least the glue was water-soluble–but they only told me that when they came home in the afternoon.

My boyfriend accidentally locked me in his room on the eighth floor, I tried to rope myself down, but the sheets weren't enough. I hung there for the last few metres waiting for the fire brigade.

I dreamt this week's lottery numbers tonight and I'm packing my bags now so I can get away really quickly with my winnings.

It's no use talking into the phone. I can't hear anything since I stood in front of the speakers at the disco last night and I'm going to the ear doctor now.

My wedding ring slipped off my finger and fell into a gully, it was quite a pain to get it out again, the lid was insanely heavy.

I got involved in a bank robbery and was completely at my wits' end. Only later did it turn out that it was the filming for a tv crime.

I think I'm starting to get Alzheimer's. First, I don't know where my house key is. Then I look for the car key. And after that I didn't know where to go at all.

Whether it's a job or school: You've overstayed your break

While I was standing outside, a car driver hit a pedestrian and I had to wait until the police had finished interviewing witnesses.

The vending machine for food vouchers was empty.

The toilet didn't flush, so I had to walk to the station *(or another building with a public toilet).*

Following the old scouting rule, I tried to help the old woman cross the road, it took forever, she put up quite a fight.

I was in town during the break and sprained my ankle. I had to sit on a bench until the worst of the pain was gone.

I got into a discussion with someone about the sense and nonsense of education. Of course, I fiercely defended the education system.

The queue in the canteen went all the way to the entrance. It took me half an hour to even get something to eat. *(Does your boss also go to the canteen? Then you should use that excuse carefully).*

I just couldn't decide what to eat.

My mobile phone battery with the time ran out during the break, of all times, so I couldn't look at the clock.

I swallowed a piece of chewing gum and had a severe coughing fit for a quarter of an hour.

I took the car to do some shopping and then couldn't find a parking space.

I went shopping during the break and there was an old woman who was carrying her bags so heavily that I carried them home for her. It was further to her than I had thought. But you know: every day a good deed.

I was almost back here when I remembered that I hadn't locked the car. So I went back to the car park.

The waitress in the café fell down with the tray full of glasses and cut herself badly–so of course I had to give first aid.

The old people's home wasn't properly locked, and suddenly dozens of confused people were blocking my way.

I stepped so stupidly into a manhole cover that I couldn't get my shoe or foot out. A passer-by then called the fire brigade, who rescued me from the awkward situation.

I was unfortunately the 100,000th visitor to the new mall and had to endure congratulations and a stupid speech.

I was shopping at the farmer's and as I was heading back into town I noticed that my smartphone was off and someone had ripped this page out of the map.

Power failure in the canteen. The food had to be reheated. I feel sick now because it tasted even more awful than normal.
I was stuck in the customer service phone queue.

I walked into a protest march of farmers and cows and promptly slipped on a cow patty. It was horrible.

I picked up an old and confused woman at the side of the road who couldn't find her way home. After an hour across the city, I gave up and delivered her to a police station.

I had to pick up something in town during my lunch break. Unfortunately, the exit barrier from the car park was defective, it just wouldn't open.

I was unfortunately held up by some strange bird, he was blabbering stupid stuff in my ear, about next week being the end of the world, some mega-rare constellation, then he blathered something about Armageddon and the beast, then I called the police, the guy belongs in a loony bin...

The vending machine for the food vouchers didn't accept the money.

I happened to meet my first husband and he had so much to say to me until his second wife came out from the hairdresser.

I had left important documents in the café and had to go all the way back again. Thank God the waitress hadn't thrown the papers away yet.

The waitress didn't come to collect the money. And I didn't want to leave without paying either.

I was still in the toilet in the pub and the toilet slogans there were so funny that I first had to recover from the laughing fit.

I had forgotten the secret number of the lock on my cupboard.

While getting food I witnessed a traffic accident and when I saw the blood I fainted.

The toilet door jammed from the inside. It took forever for someone to call the caretaker.

I am in desperate need of money, so I still had to hand in the lottery ticket, unfortunately the queue was so long. *(Does especially well when the jackpot is full again)*.

I was in the supermarket during the break when the doors were locked because tarantulas were delivered with the bananas and they all had to be caught first.

I fell into the hands of Jehovah's Witnesses in the pedestrian zone and they wouldn't let me go any further because they were trying to convert me.

Sounds like something out of a slapstick scene, but I actually slipped on a banana peel on the street and had to sit down for a while because everything hurt so much.

Believe it or not, I just got kicked by a horse.

I got into a conversation with a Star Trek fan in the canteen and fell right into the space-time continuum.

I had a muesli bar for lunch. It's supposed to bring back used energy. So I waited. To no avail.

Excuses For Your Personality And Mannerisms

The care formula for your outer appearance

I couldn't shave today because the power was out.

It's not dandruff, it's that stupid hairspray, it crumbles like that.

The stain on your trousers? That's where my scatterbrained colleague spilled the coffee on me.

Big belly? Well, I've already signed up for liposuction, but the waiting list is so long.

Funny, I never had pimples as a teenager and now I have skin problems like that, must be environmental, or maybe an allergy.

I don't want to shave my armpits because they sting so much when they grow back.

Sorry, I had a doctor's appointment and must have left my tie there.

Sorry if I smell like garlic today, but I have an awkward appointment with the boss and I want to keep it as short as possible.

My hair isn't greasy, it's hair gel.

Sorry I'm smelly, but I can't shower because of a skin rash.

Dirty shoes? Well, check out the company car park.

Unshaved? I think my three-day beard is very chic.

The weatherproof hairspray failed this morning.

If I smell something indelicate: sorry, but the public utilities turned off the water main this morning, they seem to be fixing something.

Sorry, but the deodorant doesn't live up to its advertising.

Into the bath tub? Never! I almost drowned once as a child.

Hair too long? But that's exactly the length I saw in a trend magazine the other day.

Hair removal on the legs? Why, it'll all grow back again.

The stain on the tie? How embarrassing, but in the lift some fat woman was pressing too close to me with her bag of chips and ketchup.

That's not a hairline growing out, that's a completely new colouring technique.

I always wear two different pairs of socks, it adds colour to my life.

Feel free to cultivate your idiosyncrasies

Admittedly, I can't see some things. But I refuse to wear glasses because I'm convinced they make my eyes worse.

If you can't decipher my handwriting, it's because I once had a compound fracture of my right hand as a child. Since then it always looks so scrawly.

Write a letter? I'm allergic to ink and the lead in pens.

I guess I take after my great-grandfather; he was considered very cranky.

Shaking someone's hand? But that's how you transfer a bunch of germs and get sick....

Where's the other shoe? Well, it got stuck in the door of the bus the other day.

I once read in a study that eccentrics live longer and are happier. Since then I've been trying to be an eccentric.

No, I haven't forgotten to tie my shoe laces. The reason I walk around in open-toed shoes is because my corns squeeze me so.

I know for sure, as soon as I stop smoking, I'll get cancer because I've smoked for so long. So I'd rather keep smoking.

I'm always open and say what I think. And I think it's none of your business why I am the way I am.

Against good manners. But thoroughly.

I no longer hold the door open for a woman after being yapped at so many times about it. The risk of repetition is simply too great.

Of course, a man should let women go first. But in this case, majesty goes before beauty.

I'm sorry, I can't help you into your coat, I've got it on my shoulder.

I can't shake your hand, I'm suffering from a rare contact allergy.

We live in an elbow society, so I'm afraid I can't let you go first.

Of course burping is indecent, but better to get the air out of there, right?

I'm sorry I didn't say hello to you in the street last week, but I'm short-sighted and didn't have my glasses on.

Even if the sight makes you uncomfortable–I have to mash my food to a pulp with my fork because I can't chew well with only one tooth.

I'm sorry I burp at the table, but there's something wrong with my oesophagus, it always slips out like that.

Normally I already eat with a knife and fork, but I have a strain in my left hand.

How's your figure?

My diet is completely balanced, for every packet of dark chocolate I eat a packet of white.

Diets only make me fatter.

The cake called out loudly to me. I heard it perfectly.

Well, yes, but there are preservatives in sweets and fast food and they keep me looking young longer.

Well, the more successful I became in my job, the less time I had for sport.

I don't eat much at all, but there's something wrong with my metabolism.

Oh, I've finished my beach holiday for this year, I don't want to lose weight again until next year.

I bought chocolate for the children, but it was so hot in the car that the chocolate started to melt, so I ate it myself - with the greatest reluctance, of course.

Until recently, I used to pay attention to my figure, but since there's this body positivity movement that declares a fat body a beautiful body, I now have no inhibitions about eating whatever I feel like.

If you cannot be reached by phone

The voicemail doesn't work, because I don't understand the instructions for the new mobile phone.

Oh, there was another number and voice on the answering machine? Well, my answering machine was broken and I borrowed one from the neighbours. Apparently I forgot to leave a new message.

Of course my answering machine was switched on. If it didn't switch on, then it's broken.

It's almost impossible to reach me by phone, the battery of the phone doesn't charge properly anymore.

I changed my phone provider—and since then I can hardly be reached, it's annoying!

No wonder I can hardly be reached any more, I'm almost always on the road at work. I left my mobile phone in my mother's/my sister's flat and she was away for the weekend– that's why I didn't even notice that you had left me a voicemail telling me to get in touch.

I couldn't call you back because my partner and I have the same mobile phone–and my partner accidentally plugged mine in this morning and all the numbers are in there.

There was a Mrs Meyer on the answering machine? Well, you must have dialled the wrong number.

If you cannot be reached by phone: push the answering machine forward

"This is an announcement device, all telephone lines are busy at (name), you will be connected to a recording device as soon as one becomes free again."

"You are connected. But to whom? This question is one of the great mysteries of mankind. If you can solve the mystery, please leave me a message."

"This is a secret agent AB. To prevent it from being intercepted by the enemy, it blows itself up. All you have to do is make a sound. And then I won't call you back."

"This is the machine. I'm all messed up because of all the beeping. Maybe you can still manage to leave a message."
"You are connected to No. 1234, I repeat, No. 4567, or was it 8912? Now I'm confused, please hang up and try again in an hour."

"This is the database of your online shop. After the beep, please speak your shoe size, dress size, favourite colour and monthly net income on the tape. You will receive the assortment immediately."

Successfully keeping annoying admirers at bay

Listen. My ex-boyfriend hasn't gotten over the fact that I broke up with him, and he's still so jealous that so far he's put everyone who's come near me in hospital. And I'm getting tired of nursing broken men, so we'd better drop it.

Okay, but then there's a full programme waiting for you, because my mother's tap is dripping, then you could help my uncle with the wallpapering, oh yes, and then there's my cousin, she needs some strong hands for the extension of the attic, my grandma has to be taken to the doctor from time to time, oh so and does it fit into your programme to always walk my dog in the morning?

Don't be angry with me, but I have four friends at the same time at the moment and that's stress enough.

I'm a lesbian and you won't convince me otherwise. *(Or in the other case, gay.)*

I have a boyfriend who is currently abroad for a year, but he is still the number one for me.

Since I have witnessed the many divorces among my friends, I am no longer available for a relationship.

After my hypnosis therapy I know that in my former life I was killed by my husband. Since then I refuse to have a committed relationship.

The last woman I answered had to wait two years to do so. Do you want to do the same? *(or just: "the last man I heard").*

I'm already completely booked up. Playing chess with Thomas on Mondays, music lessons with Angelo on Tuesdays, Tai Chi with David on Wednesdays, art group with Kurt on Thursdays, cinema with José on Fridays, gym with Michael on Saturdays, café with Sam on Sundays. And that every week. I really don't know where else to put you. *(Clearly, names, days of the week and leisure activities are arbitrarily interchangeable here).*

Oh no, I've outgrown the steady boyfriend age phase, it's just not that important now.

Honey, I'm constantly on the road between (put here a city far North or East) and (a city far South or West) for my job, and I don't want to have any bleating in my ear at the weekend.

It's not a good time, because I'm thinking of moving somewhere else or emigrating and I don't want to commit myself here any more.

The end of my last relationship was just eight months ago and I still have to recover from it.

Excuses for Partners, Family and Friends

How embarrassing: forgetting a birthday again

It can't be that it was your birthday, you don't look a bit older.

What? It's March already? I was still in February all this time. *(Of course: here, too, you have to change the month accordingly).*

No, I hadn't forgotten and had been trying to call all day, but either your phone or mine is out of order, it was always busy.

Sorry, but I put all the dates in the calendar which got lost last month.

I accidentally put the day in the wrong month sheet. *(So instead of May it was in June or instead of October it was in November).*

Since I took part in the memory training, I can remember names and faces better, but I can't remember any dates at all.

So this year, unfortunately, your birthday slipped through my memory, I had so much on my plate, the trouble with the boss, bullying among colleagues, then trouble with the landlord, the car broke down–I'm sorry, but these days everything really went wrong.

I didn't forget your birthday, but successfully suppressed it. I can't believe you're getting older.

Funny, but ever since I landed on a lamppost while skating, I've become more and more forgetful...

All day I thought of nothing else, but when I got home and wanted to call, there was so much trouble with the kids/ neighbours right away that it just went down.

I was so depressed because the company cut our Christmas and holiday bonuses. And on top of that, the canteen is closing. Imagine not eating at lunchtime! That's no life anymore, no wonder I have no head for other things...

My New Year's resolution for this year: to only remember the beautiful moments in life.

Oh dear, my best friend got married that day and I didn't get to make a phone call because of all the hustle and bustle.

You know, everything I don't write down, I forget. Don't take it so personally.

You just don't get any older for me.

Strange, I thought last year I wished you a week early, so this year I thought the birthday greetings would be a week later.

As nearly every year: missed the wedding day

Our relationship hasn't aged a bit, has it? It seems like a year hasn't passed since then.

Darling, I went to a dozen flower shops to buy you your favourite flowers, but I couldn't get them anywhere.

Darling, I had bought a great present on the internet and wanted to have it delivered to the office so that it would really be a surprise–but unfortunately it hasn't arrived yet.

Forgotten? No, I was just pretending, because I wanted to see if you remembered...

I wanted to look in the wedding certificate the other day, but I couldn't find it. Where did you hide it? If you didn't always put everything away...

Bunny, I have prepared a surprise, but I haven't finished it yet. Will you give me two or three more days for a really great surprise? I tell you, it will be worth the wait... That's all I'm gonna tell you right now!

Oh honey, of course I thought about the wedding day and ordered a candlelight dinner, but the fancy restaurant is completely booked up and now I've just put it down for next year. Well, then you have a whole year to look forward to it.

At the time I thought we should get married on 5.5., that would have been easier to remember. *(Could of course be 6.6, 7.7., or a similar date depending on the month).*

How could I forget the wedding day! I ordered a huge bouquet of red roses from the florist. Haven't they delivered them yet?

I'm sorry, I thought today was the anniversary. I wanted to surprise you tomorrow.

No, not forgotten at all. The embarrassing thing is: I got you something really nice as a present, but I hid it so well that I can't find it myself now.

But dearest, what does this one day count among the other 364 days of a happy marriage?

My assistant forgot to remind me.

Darling, getting married means wanting to grow older together. And part of growing older is also becoming forgetful.

Explanations for jealousy scenes, which of course lack any foundation

The lipstick on the shirt collar? Oh yes, there was a nasty jolt in the lift today and all the people fell against each other, that must have been what happened.

Yes, I know I'm coming home late, but the meeting this afternoon was so exhausting, I fell asleep in my office afterwards.

The note with the phone number? It belongs to my best friend Thomas' girlfriend. She hasn't wanted to see him for four weeks, the poor guy doesn't know why and has asked me to play the mediator, so to speak.

Do I really smell like perfume? Well, I wanted to buy you one and I went to a perfumery, but I couldn't decide at all. Just tell me which one you'd like, okay?

Of course, I'm late from the office. But the boss started a conversation about strategic planning this evening and also talked a bit about personnel policy–so I couldn't just leave.

Don't you always say I smoke too much? You see, that's why I go to a cessation group in the evenings. I just hope that the effort pays off and I really lose the desire to smoke.

Things are going haywire at the office, first my boss is ill, then his secretary, someone has to keep things running.

What do I do with these potency pills? I'm not doing anything with them, they don't belong to me, I just ordered them for my boyfriend over the internet.

The address of the escapade agency? There's a simple reason for that: a friend of mine from school days has become a journalist and he's currently doing research on infidelity agencies and has asked me to call them as a straw man.

Honey, it might be a bit late in the evenings in the next few weeks, because my boss is leaving soon and I want to be well prepared when it comes to who will take over his position.

Please don't blame me for coming home from the office so late lately. Actually, I wanted to surprise you, but please, then I'll just say it now: I'm still doing muscle-building training in the evening to get rid of the lifebuoys on my stomach. After all, I still want to please you in a few years.

The package from the sex shop that came today? I don't understand it either, someone must have ordered it in my name. Probably to make you jealous.

Maybe for a good reason: not keeping a promise.

Yes, I was going to do it, but then I told my husband about it and he offered. Hasn't he done it yet? *(Alternatively, you can use your wife, aunt, grandma, uncle or just a first name like here).*

I couldn't do it, the union is on strike and there's nothing going on at the moment.

My phone and answering machine have been switched off for a few days because someone has been terrorising me with stupid calls for the last few days.

Help in the garden to pull weeds? I don't know the difference between weeds and herbs. Maybe I'm pulling out the wrong plants.

An invitation to an evening with pictures from your last holiday? That's really lovely, but there's something wrong with my eyes, when I look intently they start to water.

No, I can't go to the cinema this week, my glasses are at the optician for repair and I can't see anything without them.

Of course, I could drive grandma to the doctor, but I've just misplaced the car keys.

Ah, the knot in the handkerchief should remind me *of this*....

Went to the cleaners today but the stain was still in it, it's going to be cleaned again now.

I can't take Auntie Frida there, my car has to go in for servicing.
I'm supposed to have said I'd take your kids to the zoo? When I'm allergic to animal hair?

Unfortunately, I can't help with the shelves, my drill broke down last week.

I'm afraid I can't go to the cinema. I've got a back problem and can't sit still for long.

There's already an extraordinary meeting of the small animal breeders' association that day.

No, I can't dig up Grandma's garden, I got lumbago yesterday.

I wanted to get your suit from the cleaners, but it wasn't ready yet. *(... Or pick up the freshly developed photos, or pick up the shoes from the shoemaker, or...)*. Pick up your suit from the cleaners? But I don't have a pick-up slip.

This week I have to work overtime because a colleague is on holiday.

52

Impossible! The Football Cup final is being broadcast that day.

Unfortunately, I can't take part in the family bike ride, my bike and I had an accident yesterday. I'm fine, but my bike is flat.

Always a hard case: not to attend the family party

Aunt Martha drives me up the wall with her wisdom–and my nervous system can't take it.

I can't, we have an important conference the next day and I have to go to bed at 8 in the evening to get a good night's sleep.

(For the last-minute cancellation:) I can't come today, my best friend's dog/hamster has died and I have to be with him now and offer support.

My horoscope predicts quarrels and separation this week—so I'd rather not come to Aunt Agnes' birthday.

No thanks, I was so sick after the last family dinner, I don't want to experience that again.

I already have an important business dinner. I can't miss that because that's when they talk about next year's promotions.

You know my dog doesn't get along with Uncle Jim's cat.

Your uncle's birthday will also be next year– but the European Football Championship *(or another important sporting event)* won't be for another four years.

I lost the crown from my incisor yesterday–I can't possibly go out in public like this.

I have a nasty stomach/ intestinal flu at the moment and wouldn't survive a feast.

I'll have to skip Christmas with the whole family this year, I have no money for presents.

My nervous stomach forbids me coffee and cake at grandma's.

I couldn't find a suitable present for Aunt Sophie and I'm not going to give myself the nerve to come with any frills. I'd rather stay at home.

I told Marcus *(or rather the name of a close relative)* I'd punch him in the nose next time we meet–should that be on Grandma's 75th birthday of all days?

My doctor has forbidden me any excitement–and Grandpa upsets me, so old and another birthday.

I have the suspicion that I am a foundling and that I don't belong to the family at all, and as long as this suspicion is not dispelled, I don't want to meet anyone's eyes.

No, I can't come. If everyone is there, it moves me so much that I have to cry, and I don't want to spoil the evening for you.

Avoiding a holiday with distant acquaintances

I can't go there, I'm extremely sensitive to the climate/to the food there.

No, I'm not in the mood for a hotel holiday, I wanted to roam around as a backpacker again.

I don't go on holiday with Tom and John. I always lose so miserably when I'm drinking. And that's all there is to this holiday.

I'm afraid I have to cancel. My boss has banned me from going on holiday this summer.

I'm sorry, but this city is always full of people and I suffer from claustrophobia.

My doctor said that a holiday in the mountains is not good for me because of my allergy to heights.

You should have said that earlier! Now we have already planned a holiday together with the neighbour family.

I'd rather save the money for the holiday so that I can have a higher pension later.

To be honest, I can't do anything with the culture and the sights in this country.

A colleague is on holiday at the same time, so I don't even need to apply.

I don't want to go there, the people in that country are too unfriendly for me.

The fine art of cooking - and the mishaps in the process

Darling, unfortunately the meal didn't turn out because you forgot the pepper the last time you went shopping, so now it's just a bit bland.

Unfortunately, I put the sugar for the dessert in the sauce and the salt in the dessert.

Hm, there's not much to eat today, I had to throw away half the potatoes because they were completely burnt. Unfortunately, there wasn't enough water in the pot.

The crispy chicken is one thing. It's crispy on the outside, but unfortunately still raw on the inside. Somehow I must have hit the temperature knob while vacuuming.

The casserole didn't turn out, somehow the cooker is defective.

The food isn't ready yet; the salad was full of snails and it took me ages to pick them all out.

The pancakes taste strange, I'm almost afraid the milk was already sour.

Darling, I'm afraid I can't make you coffee because I accidentally bought the coffee beans instead of ground coffee.

The whipped cream didn't turn out, I whisked it for minutes but it didn't get stiff. I wonder if the cream was already bad.

When I tried to cut the meat into small pieces, it was so tough that I soaked it in vinegar. Tomorrow we'll have sauerbraten and today we'll go to the Italian restaurant, okay?

I'm afraid I mixed up the paprika and the chilli powder...

Darling, the last two slices of toast are charred because the switch was set wrong. I hope you're not that hungry.

Well, it's not going to work out with the beef steaks today. The dog stole the meat from the table and ate it immediately.

The cake stayed flat. I wonder if I forgot the baking powder.

There's something wrong with the oven. First everything stayed light and when I turned up the heat, everything was black in 10 minutes.

Unfortunately, the roast potatoes look like chips, only a bit darker. I was off the cooker for a minute too long.

The meat is nice and even on both sides. Unfortunately, just evenly black. I wonder if the cooker was set too hot.

Today was a day. I was cooking when the dog came into the flat, the neighbour rang the doorbell and the children started fighting. So I burnt everything.

Too dry and bland? I followed the recipe exactly—there must be a misprint in the cookbook.

Who likes to do the housework?

Not vacuumed yet? How can you when the power's been off all day?

Honey, I can't clean up now because I have to get ready for a meeting tomorrow.

Do the laundry? Already? There's plenty of clean clothes in the wardrobe.

I was going to iron, but the iron shorted out.

I can't tidy the flat now, I have to rush to the shops.

I think the washing machine is calcified. It makes a funny crunching noise. And water doesn't come in any more either.

The hoover coughed every time, maybe it has a dust allergy.

The cleaning agent gives me a skin rash so quickly.

Look at my horoscope: Venus is in the 5th house today and Saturn in the 7th house, how am I supposed to clean the flat?

I have such a headache, I really couldn't bear the noise of the hoover now.

The washing-up liquid is bad. It didn't foam properly any more, so I poured it out.

I can't do the dishes, I cut off half my finger yesterday.

Why tidy up? I think it all looks very tidy.

I never clean because otherwise my dust mite breeding would be endangered.

Excuses for Acquaintances, Neighbourhood and Club Life

Noise protection ordinance: Excuses for the neighbourhood

The noise tonight? Oh, I see, a shelf broke down in the display case and everything got broken.

Unfortunately, it got a bit noisy last night. We had a couple over and they suddenly got into a fight, throwing plates and stuff. Our flat looks...

Did you hear the music last night? We met the artist on the outward flight on our last holiday. Really great sound, isn't it?

Sorry I was still showering at midnight, but when I opened the top kitchen cupboard, the bag of flour fell on my head.

What does the hallway look like? Oh, that's because of the dog. Normally he doesn't drool at all, but because of his stomach problems the vet gave him a medicine that unfortunately increases saliva production.

The hamster escaped from the cage and we moved all the furniture around until we caught the runaway again.

There was something going on tonight! I dropped an open packet of washing powder on the carpet, my wife rushed out of the kitchen with her glass of red wine - you can't imagine what it looked like there. We had to vacuum and scrub for hours until it was more or less okay.

Was it very loud tonight? A friend of my husband's got kicked out of his wife's house, asked to spend the night with us and then unfortunately started to rant loudly about the world in general and women in particular. We couldn't calm him down at all. Well, thank God he's back home now.

I'm sorry that the washing machine was still running last night, but I had spilled half a bottle of red wine on the tablecloth, and my mother always said red wine mustn't dry out, you have to wash it out immediately.

But that wasn't our dog barking all night.

The volume control on the stereo is broken. It always turns itself up.

I won't be able to clean the stairwell for the next few weeks because I got a nerve stuck in my back.

Dusting so late? Well, the hoover bag was full and to quickly vacuum the hallway, I taped a plastic bag to it. Well, and then the plastic bag shreds apart and the dirt through the flat. My wife was so angry that I had to spend the whole night getting all the dust out of all the nooks and crannies, otherwise she would have divorced me.

There's no such thing as unbreakable: now you need an excuse

Well, the cable from the lawn mower unfortunately broke, the lawn was so high that I didn't see it and drove over it.

The window was too clean, I thought it was open.

Unfortunately, my husband wanted to practise teeing off for golf in the living room and unfortunately he hit the TV set/other valuable item of yours with the club in the process.

I got stuck on the vase with the hoover hose.

Unfortunately I got caught in a downpour with the appliance–now it doesn't work any more, it's probably water damage ...

I wanted to chase an annoying fly with the fly swatter, but unfortunately knocked over this valuable porcelain figurine.

Unfortunately, one of the legs of the barbecue is missing because the dog tried to steal the meat and knocked over the whole barbecue. One of the legs was so bent that it couldn't be used at all.

Hm, yes, your sinfully expensive evening dress. Unfortunately, I fell into a bed of roses with it. How much was it again?

Unfortunately, I had left it on the roof of the car, it fell off while I was driving and was flattened by a 20-ton truck.

Training for the brain: weak in sports, strong in excuses

My opponent fouled all the time and the referee always missed it on purpose.

I got all the instructional films on the internet, but haven't had time to watch them all yet.

I forgot to put the spikes on *(e.g. football and track and field)*.

With me, they always put the bar up tighter than with the others. *(high jump)*

My opponent always pushed me away.

I would have easily cleared the obstacle, but the horse couldn't jump that high.

My opponent insulted me so much that I just became insecure.

I just got over a bad cold and I'm not really fit yet.

I was standing completely free and would have had the best chance of scoring, but our left winger is too blind to see something like that. *(Football)*

I was only so slow because I had put on the wrong spikes. *(Football/ Athletics)*

The grip/strings of my racket were not tight enough.

I had more headwind than the riders who started in front of me.

Something's wrong with the air pressure today, I'm really having circulation problems.

The negative vibrations of the spectators paralysed me.

I need new shoes, these were pressing on my toes so much that I could hardly run.

Since the doctor prescribed the new stomach medicine, my condition has gone down the drain.

Just as I was coming into the home straight, the wind died *(Sailing/ Windsurfing).*

Terrestrial gravity is not strong enough today.

I was still so exhausted from the marathon yesterday.

The sun blinded me so much *(Tennis etc.).*

That lame-ass referee couldn't run fast enough and therefore didn't notice the foul at all.

I couldn't concentrate properly because a death in a distant family circle was quite close to my heart.

The coach said we should bite the opponents and when I wanted to do that, my own people held me back. That's the only reason we lost.

That's a classic example of the chaos theory: somewhere a butterfly flutters its wings and here the breeze whirls the ball in the wrong direction.

Forgotten to return something you borrowed? Here is the explanation

I still need the drill because the wall looks like Swiss cheese but the shelf hooks still don't match the holes.

Return the borrowed bottle of milk? But it was already bad, so I poured it out.

My sister loved the DVD so much that she kidnapped it from me. I'll call her first thing tomorrow.

Unfortunately, the neighbour's dog peed on it, so it's at the dry cleaners.

Sure, I still have the book, but I have so much on my plate at the moment, I'm still at the beginning.

Thank you again for lending me the dress. I'll get it back to you as soon as the tailor puts the new zip in.

Can I keep your exercise bike for a while? At the moment I'm so frustrated with the boss that I'm eating like crazy. Without it, I'm falling apart like a steam ball.

I haven't been able to transfer your CD yet, my drive is spinning.

We still need the book to support the wobbly table in the cellar.

Your cough drops have really helped, my cough is completely gone. Unfortunately, the bottle is empty now too.

Unfortunately, I'm a bit fast down the hill with your bike. I'll put a new rim in for the eighth and then you'll get it back right away.

The book with the diet recipes is great. I've already lost 2 kilos with the one recipe. Can I try the other recipes too?

Your Italian dictionary came in really handy on holiday. Unfortunately, I forgot it at the hotel.

I haven't been able to pay back the money I borrowed because I haven't received my salary yet.

The adventure game on the DVD is really strong. Unfortunately, the DVD is now stuck in the drive and won't come out. I'm afraid I'll have to remove the drive first.

Your evening dress really caused a stir. Unfortunately, some idiot spilled his wine on it. So, it's at the cleaners now.

Oh, the trainers? Well, when my sister came to visit with her dog, he tore them to shreds. Must have been the smell.

Well, the hoover sucks really thoroughly, but now the bag is full, so I don't want to return it, I'll get you a new pack of bags first.

I can't return the book I borrowed until next week because I haven't been able to read it yet due to my conjunctivitis.

Excuses for School
and Study

Tolerable excuses for unbearable homework

I couldn't concentrate on homework because they were showing such violent cartoons on TV again.

My mother tried to seal the burst water pipe with the paper pages from the notebook.

My hamster died of a nasty disease yesterday and I had to fill out so many papers at the veterinary office that I couldn't write in the evening.

I did my homework, but I left it on the school bus this morning.

My sister is sick. She always does my homework.

Homework? That was supposed to be the subject matter today, wasn't it?

My brother promised to help me with my homework, but then he didn't come home last night.

Homework? We don't have a proper home!

We had to go to my great aunt's funeral yesterday and didn't get back until late.

I'm sure I did the homework, but apparently I put it in the wrong bag.

My mother tore up the homework because she said I had too many spelling mistakes. Well, she only knows the old spelling.

My brother had sunk my homework book in the aquarium and it took me three hours to blow-dry all the pages. *(Of course, the excuse works better when you can show a watered-down and blow-dried notebook.)*

I think I got something wrong there. I thought it was for tomorrow.

My word processor has an auto-text module— that must have taken on a life of its own...

I dropped the heavy dictionary on my hand and with bruised fingers I couldn't look anything up.

I tried for hours to explain the task to my father. In the end, there was no time left to do the tasks.

My mother vacuumed the keyboard. Now there are too many letters missing.

My dog swallowed the mouse ball and I'm still waiting for it to come out again.

My grandma turned 100 and no one had time to do my homework.

My screen was suddenly on fire.

My little sister probably wanted to get back at me for dyeing her rabbit pink...

The ink was empty and it's my only pen.

So that parents and teachers understand why the grade is so bad.

I don't understand, I got an A in my last paper.

I forgot to write my name on the paper and the guy next door, who is much worse than me, wrote my name on his paper. Now he says that the paper with the grade B is his paper because the paper with the E has my name on it.

I had studied for that day–but stupidly for the wrong subject.

During the maths work, it was so dull in the room that my solar calculator didn't work.

Of course I studied, but only managed 90 per cent of the material, and the test was about exactly that missing 10 per cent.

Well, if that was wrong, then the Wikipedia author made completely false statements.

I was in shock because of the film documentary the night before about the future of humanity with all the plastic waste and plasticisers in food packaging. Mankind has such big problems, all of which are home-made–this dimension made me shiver and forget any thought of this class assignment altogether.

I am too stupid for that. Which brings me to the question of whether intelligence is environmental or genetic?

That wasn't my fault. I copied the crap from the person sitting next to me.

I was bullied so much on the school bus that I was still all shaky and distracted later during classwork.

The teachers teach us this rubbish–and afterwards they say it's not like that and give bad marks.

I had studied, but during the exam I was still in shock from returning the maths paper the hour before.

At first I couldn't think of anything and then I didn't know what to do.

I couldn't learn the words because I was hoarse. And I only retain new words by reciting them out loud.

I was so excited that I had taken valerian tablets. And with those I didn't remember anything.

I couldn't study at all, because the day before, my notebook with all the notes was stolen.

The written work is not yet available

Since the keyboard didn't work, I wanted to write the homework by hand. But guess what, in the computer shop they told me that stationery is out, they don't sell any at all.

The canary tore up the notes and built a nest out of them.

My girlfriend hasn't finished typing it up yet.

Yesterday was scrap paper collection and my mother rubbished all the papers.

The printer tore the paper and I hadn't saved the document.

On the way to school, my whole bag was stolen.

My little brother made the handwritten finished work completely illegible with his chocolate fingers.

I have actually already written the last chapter, but then found an interesting document from the 18th century. I want to evaluate that first so that I can perhaps work it in.

Somthung es wrng weth te keybort, all tho lettrs arrg grong!

Suddenly all the pages were gone. I suspect the dog ate the work, because he's been constipated for two days.

I sent the only copy to the science editor of a magazine for printing and haven't got it back yet.

I don't understand that. Saturday night I dropped the paper in the mailbox here.

The stick got on this magnetic thing at the checkout while I was shopping. Now all the data is broken and I have to start all over again.

My grandfather died and my mother has been crying for days. Totally impossible to concentrate on anything with all that noise.

I couldn't do my homework yesterday because it was getting dark outside and I couldn't see anything.

Since we got this shredder at home, nothing is safe from my brother.

Hmm, I thought, as long as the copied portion is under 10 per cent, it's within the bounds of the usual.

I was rereading the paper in the car on the way to school and when my dad opens the window, leaves fly out the window. We stopped immediately, but only managed to collect a few leaves, the rest were blown away by the wind.

For days I've been searching all my trouser and jacket pockets, but the memory stick is just gone!

Everything has been going wrong for days, now I asked my astrologer yesterday and she said that with this Mars constellation I shouldn't be surprised, as long as this constellation prevails, it won't work.

Giving a presentation is avoidable

I am in therapeutic treatment for speech anxiety, giving a presentation now would jeopardise the success of the treatment.

I am so forgetful and can't even remember the topic of the presentation. And who are you?

We went to visit the aunt at the weekend and I left all the papers there. The aunt is sending me the things by post, but the package is still on its way....

How am I supposed to speak freely on this topic in a paper under such circumstances, as an unfree person who is being forced to give a speech?

Neither on Wikipedia nor on any other student website was there any information on this topic.

In the dining room there is this precious antique cupboard with the valuable crystal glasses in it. Now the base has broken off and my parents have taken the pile of paper with the concept to prop it up. Do you think I'm going to pull that out of there at the risk of it all toppling over?

I needed money for the textbooks, so I sold my paper with all the licensing rights to someone in the parallel class.

Yesterday I had put the papers on the radiator and some idiot put a bar of chocolate on it. Now look at the mess! You can't read anything anymore. *(Of course, the paper should be presented in an appropriately prepared state. In the summer, the heating doesn't work, so it was the windowsill on which the sun was shining).*

I was still missing an important textbook from the library, but when I

73

got there yesterday, it was already closed. And I can't give a presentation if I'm not one hundred percent prepared.

Give the presentation? Today? That was on the programme for next week, wasn't it?!

The speech therapist found out that I have nodules on my vocal cords. I'm not allowed to speak aloud for the next four weeks.

I'm in trouble with my father and now I'm not allowed to use the computer. I told him that I need the paper, but he thinks it's an excuse to get out of his way.

Why talk about the subject of XXX? I was told to present on YYY.

There was an emergency in the family, my grandfather had to be rushed to hospital with an asthma attack, it was really touch and go and the stress was just too much for me.

(In a croaky voice:) I'm much too hoarse, I can't talk.

Unfortunately, I packed a cooking recipe from my mother instead of the speech manuscript.

Better no grade than an F

I'm not taking notes, or do you want to be responsible for me not being admitted to medical school and therefore humanity never winning the fight against cancer thanks to my new therapeutic approach?

I have a blood test next week and wanted to study for it because I think it's important. Now I've been looking for literature in the library for the last two days and haven't found anything suitable.

I discovered that I was switched as an infant. Now I won't come to the exam because I'm not me at all, and then someone else would get my good mark.

I can't write the paper, I've only just learned to read.

I didn't take notes because this exam has nothing whatsoever to do with my career goal as a model. *(Could be a singer, actor or star photographer of course).*

The way the desk faces the window, according to feng shui teachings, a bad grade must come out. That's unfair, I can't participate like that.

I missed an important part of the class, so I had a transcript given to me, but it was completely useless for studying.

If I take notes now and get an F, my hereditary uncle will cut me out of his will. Do you want to be responsible for that?

I fell on my right wrist last night while doing sport, and I can't write with my left.

I can't take notes. My lucky pencil is gone.

Overslept or unfocused? Here is the explanation:

I accidentally took the sleeping pills instead of the vitamin pills this morning.

I went to the dentist and he gave me too high a dose of anaesthetic.

Since my hamster died, I can't think of anything else because of my grief.

I studied all night for the exam in the next lesson.

I think it's the cough drops. There's something I can't take.

Ever since I hit the wall while skating, I've had such a funny feeling in my head.

The last blood test revealed an iron deficiency. That's why my head doesn't get enough oxygen and I'm always so tired.

I couldn't keep up with the work because I lost my cheat sheet.

I go to work at night to be able to afford all the textbooks.

My big brother hit me so hard last night that I still feel woozy today.

Just now, in chemistry class, I felt so funny when I tried to do it. And since then I haven't come to at all. I wonder if it's an allergic reaction to my biochemistry.

The people in the flat next door were bickering all night, so I couldn't sleep at all.

Brain jogging against school sports

I ate too many beans, so if I run now, the others in the gym won't be able to breathe.

At the risk of sounding like a stupid excuse, I forgot my trainers at home in the rush this morning.

I feel sick. Really sick.

I still have sore muscles from tonight. *(When asked what was going on, the answer might be: training for the Iron Man, exhausted while dancing or lifted glasses).*

My mum didn't sew the gym shorts yesterday and with the huge tear in the crotch I can't wear them like this.

My doctor has forbidden me to sweat because of the athlete's foot.

I just had a bad fall on the stairs–I can't possibly go with this strain.

(For swimming lessons): Yesterday I had a past life regression. It came out that I went down with the Titanic. You will understand that I am not able to go into the water again today.

(For swimming lessons): I protest against the senseless killing of numerous micro-organisms by chlorinated water.

I can't join in because if I break a sweat it will ruin my hairstyle, and what do you think my mother says when she has paid so much money for a senselessly ruined hairstyle?

When I was stretching, I sprained something in my cervical spine and now I can't move my head.

I have an appointment at the dermatologist for a big allergy test and I mustn't start sweating now, otherwise the result will be falsified.

I forgot to cut my toenails and now I can't get into my trainers.

My athlete's foot hasn't completely healed and I don't want to infect the others in the swimming pool.

Because I don't get any more pocket money from my parents, I've gone on an indefinite strike. I'd love to join, but then you have to negotiate with my parents for that.

My mother washed all the sports clothes yesterday, but didn't put them in the dryer. This morning everything was still wet.

My sense of balance is not okay. As soon as I walk a bit faster, turn or jump, I get totally dizzy, so I can't participate.

Excuses For
Bosses & Colleagues

You have not yet completed your most urgent task

Where is this QM manual with the regulations?

Please do not speak to me now. I am in the process of finding a solution to our communication problem.

I have just rethought the assignment to come up with a solution in a shorter time.

I've been so forgetful lately... What am I actually doing here? And who are you anyway?

First I had to look up in the quality assurance manual what to do in order to carry out this task according to ISO standards.

I had forgotten to write it down on the note with the urgent tasks.

Sorry, I didn't hear that this morning. My tinnitus is whistling so loud again today. *(With tinnitus, you have loud, annoying noises in your ear. Unfortunately, all the time. So you should think carefully about whether you really take this excuse).*

It was due at eleven? Hmm, the battery of my watch seems to be weak, just now it was half past nine.

The task can't be done in this short time.

Someone must have taken my calendar.

I'm doing a deep hypnosis for self-discovery. And those who find themselves also find everything else, for example the solution to urgent problems.

With all the complaints here, I don't have time for that anymore.

I'm brain blond, I couldn't remember that.

Spring awakening all around me–and I'm supposed to be able to concentrate on the mundane bookkeeping?

I still need the approval of the management.

The operating instructions have disappeared. How am I supposed to work properly?

I can't find this procedure in the QM manual.

It's never been done this quickly before.

Mrs Smith always wants to make a name for herself. Let her have a go.

I don't know what you want. I didn't find this word in the dictionary. Can you please explain it again in dictionary terms?

The backup of the data is no longer to be found.

For five hours and twenty-four minutes I've been stuck on the software company's telephone hotline...

You know: good things take time.

Sorry, my neural network is having routing problems at the moment.

You are completely sleepy or unfocused

I have not been sleeping, but meditating on the problem. Five more minutes and I'd have the solution.

I have an allergic reaction to the printer toner, my blood no longer transports enough oxygen.

Haven't you noticed yet that the coffee machine is broken?

For a few days now I've been sleepwalking at night and during the day I just don't have enough energy.

It's the electro-smog, no wonder with all the appliances here.

My goodness, the flu medicine has scary side effects...

That's power napping, the secret of success of the real top managers. Didn't you know about it?

I was bitten by a tsetse fly on my last holiday. *(The tsetse fly is the carrier of the so-called sleeping sickness, but to be bitten by it you have to have been in Africa).*

Have you ever taken Viagra? No? See, then you don't understand this either.

This is to compensate for the six hours I spent tonight on strategic planning.

I don't sleep at my desk at all, my cervical spine is so messed up that my physiotherapist has recommended I put my head on the desk top several times a day.

Ever since they put up the radio mast in the neighbourhood, I've been so dizzy.

Is it possible that they've been making decaffeinated coffee here for the last few days?

It's no wonder, the office furnishings contradict all Feng Shui rules.

Someone must have put sleeping pills in my coffee. That's almost like sabotage.

The nylon stockings today are statically charged and interfere with the electrical transmission of stimuli in the brain.

It's just the highly concentrated 15-minute power break we were taught at the last management seminar.

It must be the ozone emanating from office equipment.

My biorhythm is running prematurely, you should have seen me at 6am this morning, I was full of beans.

My head was on the desk top because a contact lens fell out. I thought, the closer I am to the desk, the more likely I am to see it.

This is a highly effective yoga exercise to relieve work stress. Works well, you should try it too.

You have not delivered something

I am still waiting for your approval, I have already told you that.

I had arranged it, Ms XXX wanted to do it for me.

Apparently I'm starting to get Alzheimer's now, well, it started much earlier with my grandparents and parents.

I've already sent it out via the intranet, if it hasn't arrived yet, it must have got stuck somewhere.

My former boss never asked me to do that.

I'm afraid of all the redundancies, and this fear totally paralyses me. I really need to see a psychotherapist, I can't go on like this.

This is my burn-out again.

I'm sorry, but the prosthesis of my left brain is currently at its annual check-up.

You didn't mention that task at the interview.

I've been so busy, I haven't gotten around to it. Maybe a position should be created after all.

I just did that last week, is that due again?

I never got the job.

I was just about to start when there was a test alarm. You didn't hear anything??? I'll have to see an ear doctor. Maybe I have tinnitus.

Use the pitfalls of technology

Apart from general protection violations, the computer does nothing today.

Since things are getting worse with global warming, this computer is going slower and slower.

The printer goes haywire: the continuous paper it is printing on can only be used as toilet paper.

The cleaning lady must have loosened a cable while cleaning, with this tangle of cables I just haven't figured out which one yet.

With this new appliance came an instruction manual that is completely incomprehensible.

I didn't get into the folder, could it be that the server is down right now?

There was a paper jam in the copier, when I got it out the paper tore and it took forever to fish out the little snippets.

I don't know what it is, the colleague from IT muttered something in his beard, sounded like a Doppler effect.

Since the new hard drive has been in, there are always some kind of routing problems.

The copier is so slow today, I think it needs maintenance again.

The monitor keeps saying "Insert a coin", but I don't know where.

Well, unfortunately I forgot the password and now I can't get to the documents.

I think my PC is bullying me. It can only be intentional if it doesn't want to work.

What? My mail had "You giant dumbass" in the subject line? There must have been a virus infecting the mail programme...

Since the box has been tuned, I can't get the Excel curves to work as quickly. Is there a spoiler missing?

The monitor has been so strange lately. I wonder if it needs a few new pixels.

The motherboard is also a bit older now and is taking longer and longer lunch breaks.

Some colleague is keeping the server busy calculating the highest probability for the next lottery numbers.

Someone has fiddled with my screen display and now I don't recognise anything.

There's something wrong with the mouse cable, I can't click on anything anymore, I always miss.

It doesn't work and I wanted to call the developers of Windows, but do you think I'll ever get through there in Seattle? It's just bad customer service.

You are playing on the computer or surfing the Internet privately

What you have just seen is a new, energy-saving screen saver.

You don't think I'm playing, do you? This is a training to better coordinate the right and left hemispheres of the brain. After that, you work much more productively.

I'm looking for a new report on benchmarking in Japan. I don't know how I got there.

It's a game that professionals use to train concentration, problem-solving and assertiveness.

I'm currently reading up on viral marketing 5,0, which is the trend of the future.

I almost think I have a virus on my hard drive. Should I tell the IT department?

I'm reading up on the latest trends in the market.

Yes, our competitors' websites are much more colourful and flashy. We should rethink our marketing strategy.

I have no idea what that is. The USB stick said "clients 2019". These are probably still files from my predecessor.

No, I'm not doing this privately, instead this is about getting into the lifestyle of the under-30 target group. I myself am already out of the age for these games...

My therapist said that playing games is good for relieving stress.

How do I gloss over unattractive things in job applications?

The notice of termination is for the employment agency. In reality, the contract was cancelled by mutual agreement. ***

Computer skills? Of course. I always turned off my colleague's monitor so it wouldn't run so hot.

The job at the rubbish collection? I only did that to support a journalist in his investigative research.

Hobbies? I work so much all the time, there's no time at all for them.

That's not a disadvantage to have changed jobs so often— it's more a sign of flexibility and a high degree of willingness to adapt.

Of course, I am friendly when dealing with customers. Even when they complain about the company, the boss and the goods.

Since so many companies have to increase their quota of women, it's hard for a man to get a good position despite having the best qualifications...

Why did I start a second apprenticeship after my first? Quite simply to prepare myself for working life in as many different ways as possible.

Dealing with superiors? Well, it wasn't so good in the last company because the boss was always throwing the phone at us. You really get scared when you have such outbursts of rage.

At the time, my tax advisor said I earned too much, so I switched to the job at the fast food restaurant.

Yes, there is a gap in my CV. During this time I was abroad and expanded my social skills, also in dealing with foreign cultures.

The fact that I've worked for thirteen different companies in the last six months is just proof that they were courting me.

No, the "was always on time" cannot be meant ironically, I was always the first one on the job.

Even though I had previously worked as a night porter–but during that time I acquired essential key qualifications.

Software skills? Well, as long as I don't have to write you a programme that can predict tomorrow's lottery numbers or stock market prices....

You're saying that "met expectations" in the reference is a bad evaluation? Well, you know, my ex-boss is a good craftsman, but he doesn't know the secrets of the language of references. He meant it in a positive way.

Excuses For Customers & Business Partners

The client's order has not yet been completed

I'm still waiting for approval from the boss, but he's in an important meeting.

Was that urgent? You didn't say that clearly enough.

I had taken care of it, but then the coffee machine exploded and messed everything up.

That's never happened in our company before, the fault must lie elsewhere.

Since the boss ordered the new spelling, we need hours to look up all the words again. Totally impractical, but unfortunately it's an order.

I've made a note in my diary for next 29 February.

I am sorry. I wanted to, but the company's internal overtime regulations have prevented that so far.

Sorry, I misunderstood you.

It will take a little longer. My colleague has started reformatting all the hard drives.

I was trapped in the lift for hours.

The computer keyboard is somehow wrongly polarised today. I haven't been able to type anything yet without the computer crashing.

Sorry, but the admin hasn't given me the right password yet.

Sorry, my neural network is having routing problems today.

The customer has not received the goods

I could not enter the order, there is a delivery block here.

The (ship/flight) captain/ truck driver has fallen ill and with the shortage of skilled workers, a replacement is not available quickly.

The item is currently not available–haven't you been informed of this yet?

I'll have to ask at the gate. *(Possible places are, depending on the company organisation, also the shipping department or the forwarding agency.)*

Our raw material supplier has obviously not yet grasped the just-in-time concept.

Our supplier's warehouse burnt down.

The crew of the freighter has yellow fever and the ship is under quarantine.

I don't understand that. The shipping company has already delivered it. Wasn't it at your place?

I just got a call from our mechanic, he's lying on the road with the delivery van and a broken axle, waiting for the towing service. I don't think it'll work out today.

Our wholesaler doesn't have it in stock at the moment.

The staff went on strike because of the bad canteen food.

The goods are still in some port because they haven't been cleared through customs yet.

The container was mixed up, it is now on its way to the port of Hamburg.

The freight lift is defective and we can't get your goods out because of the danger of falling.

The test lab/technical department has not yet released the goods.

Our supply chain is stuck, we are now looking for new suppliers.

The delivery is late

The student trainee was smoking in the warehouse and then the sprinkler system flooded everything.

The delivery notes were printed incorrectly, so we couldn't send anything on.

The delivery was accidentally loaded onto the wrong truck, but don't worry, it's already on its way back from Bucharest.

Quality Assurance first had to check whether the speed of the delivery met the ISO standard. And that took time.

You never replied to our query about the delivery date.

The truck with your cargo was stopped at the border, imagine: the driver was an internationally wanted terrorist.

The man with the outgoing goods stamp is on holiday.

The canteen food was bad and the shipping department is completely sick at home.

We have communication problems with the supplier in China. They produced the goods the wrong way round. So, we have to start all over again.

We realised too late that the raw materials used were not of the usual quality. And since we only sell good quality, it is produced again.

We even received the goods too late from the manufacturer. Just-in-time doesn't work that way yet.

You have not called back

During the maintenance work, a technician connected the cable incorrectly.

My colleague forgot to let me know.

We had a fault in the telephone system all morning.

My co-worker is on holiday and has locked all her business cards with phone numbers in her desk.

My colleague entered the callback for the wrong day.

Billions are invested in telephone lines and the network breaks down in our neighbourhood of all places.

No, I didn't forget to call you, but I had to check something with the boss first.

The new telephone system is so complicated and I can't find the operating instructions.

Directory enquiries are still looking for your number to call you back.

The street was dug up and all the cable lines were torn apart.

I'm sorry, I even had the apprentice remind me and then he forgot.

The gas pipes in our street have been relaid and something must have been mixed up. Every time I pick up the phone, there's a detonation next door.

Could it be that the mail is stuck in the spam filter?

This morning I saw that the mail was stuck in the outbox–I'm still looking for the error.

There was no attachment to the mail–maybe it was removed by the virus killer.

I would love to help you, but after the last computer crash I'm not even allowed near the PCs now.

My colleague is stuck in the printer with his tie, we can't print anything at the moment.

I had to dig through a mountain of complaints first.

The letter is here in front of me; it came back because the postcode was wrong.

I have to check with the courier service first.

Letter/email has not arrived

I have just heard from our provider that the server has been switched off because of an unpaid bill.

The mail was routed via China—and you know, there is increasingly strict censorship there.

Well, you know—always this traffic jam on the information highway.

There's a thunderstorm here, so we've all switched off the PCs. I can't write anything until tomorrow.

Our fax machine is older and the fax roll must have been empty that day.

Some joker here has deleted all the documents on the server.

The invoice is not yet paid

The department is moving and the computers/records are not available until next Monday.

We have already sent a record of this to the relevant department.

The account number was filled in incorrectly, the bank transferred the amount back because they could not locate the recipient bank.

The goods were not received here at all.

The boss took the money to the bank but invested it badly there—he put it all on the wrong numbers.

The invoice was in the "done" folder—and if it's in there, it's done.

The accounting department said there was still an open credit note.

Because of the huge budget cuts, this payment was no longer in there.

By mistake the invoice ended up with the tax advisor / in the wrong department.

Our trainee threw all the old invoices in the shredder and added a whole pile of new invoices. Yours was probably among them. Can you send them again?

Who ordered the goods? I don't have any records of it, so I can't release the payment.

The invoices go into the payment lottery every week. Unfortunately, yours hasn't been drawn yet. Maybe next week.

We returned the merchandise. Didn't you book it?

An important signature is still missing—but the colleague is on holiday at the moment.

Unfortunately, we can't find the invoice. Can you send it again?

Why has the invoice not yet been paid? You'll have to ask our bank.

We have a much longer payment term!

Could you please send me the account statement?

What's the problem? We have offset the receivables against the liabilities.

Unfortunately, the chief accountant is ill, so nothing works in the department now.

Somehow the new software always confuses euros and dollars with cents and then nothing works.

Someone entered the wrong payment term.

The accounting department is still looking for the account assignment stamp.

The usual suspects: Problems with the computers

Our EDP is currently checking the Internet for viruses, so our computers will remain switched off today.

Due to a system change, we can't access data older than three days at the moment. The EDP is now working on fixing the error.

The computer mouse escaped.

We have a new distribution software, but we haven't been trained on it yet. Our department is supposed to get this training in three weeks.

The system administrator has a virus that has not yet been removed.

Some hackers from China have paralysed our system in order to get hold of secret company information.

We have been hearing for three days that the service is working on this problem. That's all I can tell you.

Well, you know where EDP comes from: Either "Everyone Develops Plans" or "Extremely Disturbed Programmes" or something like that.

Someone tried to calculate Pi down to the last digit. The computer's still recalculating.

All I'm getting is messages with a read-only hint. I don't know what the computer is trying to tell me...

As far as I understand, there are no more bits and bytes and the next delivery will come next week.

Since yesterday afternoon we have no network connection– and therefore no access to the server with all the data.

Someone has set Chinese as the system language. Now we only have these strange characters on the screen and nobody knows how to get our Latin letters back.

Our IT representative forgot the system password. Now nothing works.

Our firewall had to be deleted.

The hard disk reports defective sectors. The boss is getting a screwdriver to take a look at them. My colleague is still trying to convince him to call the service. Otherwise the box will probably never run again.

The monitor is missing a few pixels on the bottom right. Now it no longer shows the most important numbers.

The air-conditioning in the computer centre has failed and the computers are running hot.

Your colleague/chief cannot be reached by phone

Unfortunately, I can't connect you to him at the moment, he swallowed a cough drop earlier and since then he can't make a sound.

The boss is on the run from the tax office.

He has a meeting with his superior, you will understand that I cannot disturb him.

My colleague's phone system is down right now, the technician is working on it, but it will probably take a while.

He/she is at a seminar for good personnel management.

I cannot connect you with him, the boss was sacked yesterday.

I'm sorry, the department heads are not available because they are in a conference to find a solution to why they are so hard to reach.

He has a meeting with a big bank to secure the majority of shares in this car company.

There's no way you can talk to him again today, because when he saw how cheap we are compared to the competition, he was speechless. Try again tomorrow, maybe he will have recovered from the shock.

He has important papers in his car, which he is collecting right now. Unfortunately, he couldn't find a parking space right in front of the entrance today, so it might take a little longer.

He/she is currently at the seminar "How to make my customers happy and satisfied".

At the moment there is a meeting about the future of company communication.

He/she is having a gigantic creative period and must not be disturbed.

I can't connect you to him/her, the cleaning lady broke the phone.

He/she is at the trade fair about the office communication of tomorrow.

The boss is so busy with process optimisation that he/she is measuring the time-saving potential with the stopwatch in front of the toilets today.

The head of department is currently busy benchmarking the coffee machines in the canteen.

It's inconvenient at the moment, the gentlemen from the tax investigation are in there with him right now.

At the moment, he has a staff meeting with the little blonde from the dispatch department.

Who do you want? He doesn't exist here.

She's on a bank call and it's about a big transaction, I can't disturb her.

My colleague is on her way to the post office. Yes, she did that yesterday too. She does it every day.

Excuses For Authorities, Institutions And Companies

How do I explain the unpaid bill?

Oh, was the letter from you an invoice? I put that in the waste paper box last week.

The letterbox at the bank was taped shut last week evening, I couldn't post the transfer.

I misplaced my glasses and the writing was so small.

I lost the papers and can't identify myself at the bank.

Some youths dented the letterbox so badly at night that the flap wouldn't open. It took quite a while before the caretaker took care of it.

I lost my mobile phone and without it I can't get a TAN number to transfer money.

I can't pay the bill until I find it again. Without it, I'm missing all my bank account details.

My child used the bill to colour and afterwards you couldn't read your address or bank details.

I thought my husband gave you a direct debit mandate....

I thought that in exchange for my silence, it would be paid out of a black fund of the–what was their name, that party?–paid for.

You know, I never pay the bills straight away, I collect them in a big box and once a month I pull one out and it gets paid straight away. If you didn't this month, maybe you'll have better luck next month.

Bill? None arrived here. When is it supposed to be from?

I thought my husband/ wife had already sorted it out.

I paid the bill via online banking. I wonder if maybe the money transfer didn't work because of some computer error.

My bank had no more forms. And I don't pay via computer on principle.

I paid, but the account number was obviously wrong, the money was charged back again.

With all these bank mergers, it makes me so confused that now I don't even know which is my bank.

This month I'm paying the bills of companies whose names are between A and G. I'm not even sure which one. Your company is next month.

Since my husband got this shredder, nothing is safe from him.

Unfortunately, the mobile TAN was sent to the wrong mobile phone and then the transfer process was cancelled.

I wanted to transfer money at the ATM, and then the box broke and swallowed my card. Now I have to go to the bank during opening hours, but there's so much going on in the shop that I can't miss it.

My accountant always does all that and he disappeared without a trace.

I wanted to go to the bank, but the queue was as long as at the social security office. And I didn't have that much time.

I wanted to add it to the next statement.

I never pay on days ending in "y".

The transfer didn't arrive? I always knew you couldn't trust online banking.

Oh, the bill was in euros *(or another currency)*? I thought it was in cents.

Well, my dog has now unfortunately acquired a taste for 80 g paper.

I can't pay because I don't know my husband's PIN. And he's in a coma in hospital.

It won't work this month. The day before yesterday I took a thousand euros (or another currency) out of my savings account to finally pay all my outstanding bills and on the way home I was robbed. Now I have nothing left for this month.

How do I explain my traffic sins?

Funny, my speedometer only showed 50 km/h *(or the speed in miles per hour)*. I wonder if it's stuck.

I have to hurry to the office, I have an important phone call coming up, it's about a project worth millions, please send me the ticket and don't keep me any longer.

Why has my MOT expired? Well, take a look: the writing on the stamp is so small—how am I supposed to read it without my glasses?

I was only trying to follow the car in which the handbag thief was fleeing. Now he's slipped through my fingers. With 500 euros *(or another currency)*!

Why are the tyres worn? I only had them put on last year.

The one-way sign was obscured by a tree.

Wrong way down a one-way street? My navigation system told me I had to go through.

I gotta get my wife to the hospital real fast. Hey? Where's my wife? Shit, I knew I forgot something.

The car with the high beams behind me blinded me, so I slowly picked up speed.

Just a few minutes ago I had to take a laxative, please let me drive on really fast or something bad will happen.

It wasn't me who was too fast—the car in front of me was too slow!

Road signs? There was so much fog, I couldn't see any...

I saw a UFO and lost my composure for a second. Only when it flashed did I realise that I was going too fast.

Well, I missed the red light because I was so dazzled by the blonde in the car on the right.

Okay, after the eleventh beer I didn't pay much attention to the blood alcohol level.

I just wanted to test if your radar worked. What do you say? 75 km/h? *(or the speed in miles per hour.)* Well, that's exactly right.

Why was I driving backwards on a one-way street? Because I couldn't go forward. Someone was holding up all the traffic.

It wasn't me who triggered the speed trap, it was the low-flying sports plane that was flying on behind me...

Someone was tailgating me so closely that I must have unconsciously been speeding up.

Driving too fast? Well, maybe, I dropped my cigarette on the seat and went a little higher with my butt to grab it, and I probably stepped on the accelerator too hard.

No overtaking? Yes, but the rear fog light of the car in front of me was so bright in these light conditions that I simply had to overtake.

The blood alcohol level? Well, 1.3 would be great for a school grade.

The red light? I didn't see any, the truck in front of me was too high.

Too fast? Do you know how fast I have to go to the bathroom? I'm fighting this stomach bug that's going around...

Driving licence? You must still have it... You haven't lost it, have you?

Due to a sudden sneezing attack, the pressure on the accelerator increased and therefore I was briefly too fast for five seconds.

My mother/wife called to say that my grandpa/hamster is dying, I have to hurry home to say goodbye.

First-aid kit, warning triangle and waistcoat? That's still at a mate's. Yesterday, I helped with the move and put them next to each other for loading–and then forgot to load them again.

During the thunderstorm, the lightning blinded me, it must have been right where the speed limit sign was.

Cycling on the pavement is forbidden? But I can't manage to ride on the street anymore, ever since I was hit by a car once. I'm already in therapy for it, but it will take a while before I can cope with it nervously ...

Pay for this ugly photo? It's not even good enough for an identity card.

You have to be completely sober about the blood-alcohol level.

How do I explain the parking violation to the traffic office?

I could swear that the sign wasn't there earlier.

(With a smile or a twinkle in the eye:) I am a woman.

The traffic sign wasn't sufficiently illuminated in the dark last night, so I couldn't see it.

I'm not parking here at all– my car is there because it jerks and sputters and I've left it there makeshift to call the garage.

Why park the wrong way? I have a bad back and park properly when I can get the door open far enough to get out of the car.

The sign wasn't there earlier, because a lorry was parked there.

I had to park the car here urgently, the dog was sick from driving and about to vomit.

I only parked the car here briefly to help an old woman over there across the cross street. That only took three minutes.

I work part-time as a press reporter and when I saw a man biting a dog, I just had to quickly park the car to photograph it.

I just quickly looked for a public toilet.

Must be the full moon tonight.

I had a parking ticket in my car. Unfortunately, it had been broken into and someone had emptied the car. And stupidly took the parking ticket as well.

I wasn't. Someone must have faked my number plate.

I misread the parking time by an hour.

Three minutes couldn't possibly have gone by.

Are you the meter maid? Nice of you to come. Maybe you can give me some change for the machine.

I was looking for someone who could change the 10 euros *(or another currency)* into small change for me.

That traffic sign back there? I'm not from here...

I just wanted to ask for directions.

The sun was blinding me, I couldn't see the sign.

I'm blonde, that explains everything, doesn't it?

How do I explain driving without a valid ticket?

I thought you didn't have to pay for standing room.

(Show a youth hostel or other ID card and say:) This is a ...-ID card with integrated network card.

I belong to a free church and my faith forbids me to pay for local public transport.

All this time I've been waiting for the conductor to pay for it.

My therapist told me to free myself from all compulsions - and a ticket is a compulsion, isn't it?

Didn't the mayor say during the last election he wants free rides for free citizens. I am a free citizen!

I'm chasing the pickpocket who stole my wallet. He's sitting in the front of the tram.

I was travelling with a few people and a group ticket and didn't manage to get off in time when I changed trains. Julia got the ticket.

The machine was overflowing, there was no more room for my money.

I travel with my husband. He has both tickets and I lost him.

I find paying at the machine so impersonal– I'd rather do it with someone like you.

Before I pay for something, I first see if I am happy with the service and the service here is bad.

I can't read the signs without my glasses. The driver drives so badly, you can't charge money for that.

There was something in the newspaper about special days with free rides.

Because of the online crime, I wanted to pay by cheque instead of cash, but that didn't work at the machine.

Don't they pay on arrival, like taxis?

I don't have my monthly travel pass with me.

I didn't want to take a ride, I just wanted to look at the fabric of the seat cushions–but as soon as I got in, the ride started.

The card machine kept spitting out the money.

Write on a sign: I'm a sleepwalker, please don't talk to me or I'll get a shock.

How do I explain the mishap or accident to the insurance company?

A gust of wind blew a piece of newspaper onto my windscreen. I didn't see anything for two seconds and that's when the accident happened.

All of a sudden the car was on the road, it must have been invisible before.

While trying to swat the annoying fly to death in the car, I must not have been paying attention to the road for a moment.

A car came out of the fog, hit mine and disappeared just as nebulously.

The man kept provoking my dog by grimacing until my dog bit him.

When I walked through the glass door, I didn't have my glasses on.

The dog was playing with the cable of the hi-fi system.

A wasp was suddenly in the car and made me completely nervous.

Our belly dance group was practising for the next performance—somehow I knocked over the vase.

The pedestrian was all indecisive about which direction to take, which was the only reason I hit him.

I didn't knock the woman over; I just ran past; the woman fell over because of the draught.

A child knocked over the vase. I just don't know which of my seven.

The cat was hunting flies and cleared the windowsill in the process.

I had the umbrella next to me on the passenger seat and when I went to reach for the biscuits next to it, I must have hit the release button, the umbrella opened and I couldn't see anything.

I am red-green-blind and unfortunately the car was red.

I only caught the pedestrian because I had to avoid the car in front of me.

There was a spider on the wall and I threw the newspaper at it but only hit the vase.

As I approached the intersection, there was suddenly a stop sign that hadn't been there last week, and I was so surprised by that that I couldn't brake in time.

I only hit the post because it was previously hidden by all the pedestrians.

My jacket was so tight in the shoulders that I couldn't turn around far enough when I parked.

I suddenly caught sight of my mother-in-law on the other side of the road and then lost control of the car.

There was a huge tanker in front of me and I was pulled over the red light by its breeze.

I looked behind and there was nothing to see and suddenly I hit the road sign.

How can the waiting time at the doctor, hairdresser or supermarket checkout be shortened?

The food is already on the cooker and will otherwise burn.

My lunch break is almost over.

My husband is waiting outside in the car and gets so irascible when he has to wait a long time.

My nanny didn't come.

Please let me go first, I get anxious around people.

I'm only going out for a minute because a repairman is coming to do the washing machine.

I can't stand the air in doctors' surgeries, I always get sick straight away.

My bus is about to leave and the next one doesn't leave for two hours. *(Alternatively, it could be the tram, the train or a plane).*

I have to go home soon, my youngest is sick in bed, I just need a prescription. *(Or in the supermarket: need to make something to eat quickly).*

I can't leave my dog alone in the flat for long, he'll tear up the sofa.

I have a chicken in the oven and it gets so tough otherwise.

I have an intestinal infection and have to get home to the toilet quickly.

My car is parked in a no-parking zone.

112

Excuses For
The Brave

Do you think anyone will believe you? Excuses why you are not yet rich and famous

I once bet on an outsider at a horse race, he even won and the betting odds were unique. But I couldn't find the ticket and so I couldn't collect all the money. That's life.

Maybe I would be on the board of IBM today if I hadn't been judged so badly by this begrudging department head. At some point I got fed up with the bullying and changed companies.

As a pupil I had played in a theatre group and had already been offered a real role, but then I started studying. Who knows if I wouldn't have become famous...

I used to play in a band, we had a great record deal and we even went on tour as the opening act for the Stones. Unfortunately, there was a fight with the lead singer and the band broke up. Otherwise we would have become a newcomer band, the Stones looked pretty old next to us.

At work a few years ago, I developed a device for energy conservation. Unfortunately the plans were stolen.

I was a top basketball player as a young kid, but then at 13 I just didn't grow up.

Actually, I was supposed to double *(name actor)* in those great scenes of *(name feature film)* many years ago, but stupidly I broke my ankle skiing and couldn't get in front of the camera with a cast.

In the 60s I met the Beatles in Hamburg and John wanted me to be their manager, but unfortunately Paul was against it. *(If the 60s are too far back for your age, pick another decade with another band).*

My violin teacher predicted a great future for me. Unfortunately, I broke my hand when I was 10 and never regained the necessary mobility.

At university I did a great research project, but the professor's assistant sold it to him as his own achievement. And now he's a professor at Harvard. But there you see again that you can only get ahead through intrigue.

If I hadn't already been married to my husband when I met George Clooney, I would have become Mrs. Clooney.

Do you remember the successful car ad campaign? Well, you know... The idea actually came from me, on holiday two years ago I met the guys from the advertising agency, we had a drink together and at a late hour I told them this spontaneous idea. What could I have earned if I had been involved in the deal?

My family would be incredibly rich today, my grandfather inherited a pile of Coca-Cola shares and sold them straight away because nobody knew Coca-Cola back then. Today they would be worth a fortune.

My grandparents had enormous estates, but they sold them for peanuts shortly after the war. Today there are industrial plants and the land is worth millions.

I was once approached in a bistro in Paris at night by a strange guy who asked me if I wanted to work as a model. I didn't like the guy at all, so I refused. When he left, someone told me it was Karl Lagerfeld.

I once filled out a lottery ticket with the right numbers—and then my wife forgot to hand it in!

Well, with my birth constellation and Mars in the 13th house, it couldn't work.

A few years ago, I developed a device for saving energy in production, the company then applied for a patent and fobbed me off with 10,000 bucks. In the meantime, there are worldwide licences and millions in sales. Well, tough luck.

I was already in front of the camera for commercials as a toddler and with my talent I would already be a star, but my father said at that time that school was more important.

Back when I was studying in the US, I told a nice guy called Jeff about my idea with the internet book mail order business. Today, Jeff is one of the richest men in the world thanks to this online bookseller.

In the 1950s, my grandfather developed a drug for a pharmaceutical company that is still widely sold today. Can you imagine that he was fobbed off with a 300 dollar bonus back then? That was it for the wealth.

116

I had once made a great invention, the bagless hoover, but at the patent office they lost my documents and by the time it was cleared up, someone else had already applied for the patent.

I wanted to buy IBM shares at the end of the 1980s and would be filthy rich today, but my banker said at the time that computing had no future.

I would be a gifted concert pianist today if my piano teacher had encouraged me properly.

It's staggering. In genetic research they have found an unlucky streak gene in humans. And I, of all people, am a carrier of this gene. That explains a lot in my biography.

I once found an old, kitschy painting in my grandmother's estate and sold it at the flea market for 50 euros *(or another currency)*. Later I saw it in the newspaper - it was a famous painter and worth 500,000.

Well, the first million didn't work out, but now I'm working on the second try.

No one will believe you: excuses from the realm of fantasy

A voice from beyond told me to stay in bed or the whole world would end.

Last night, Jesus and Buddha suddenly stood in my room and discussed their ethical approaches with me all night long. That's why I totally overslept this morning. But I know now.

I'm on my way to the nearest marine archaeology institute. Last night in a dream I was given by an ancient man the coordinates of where Atlantis sank with its gold.

I had to extend my holiday: first there was a typhoon, then the hotel was washed away by the tidal wave of a seaquake and then I couldn't find my plane ticket.

I fell into a time hole in the dream and couldn't find my way out.

Elvis is alive! I met him in town last night and that's why I'm so late.

Incredibly, I was on holiday in the US and didn't know that New Hampshire had a law forbidding people to nod their heads or tap their feet to the beats of music. And I did just that in a coffee shop and got arrested. By the time I got out, my return flight had been forfeited, I had a lot of trouble with the authorities and the airline, well in short: I was in the States three weeks longer than planned.

I woke up this morning and was tied to my bed with invisible ropes. I couldn't even move my big toe.

I'm sorry I'm late, my spaceship was delayed. Somehow it missed its departure at the last galaxy.

A carpet dealer wanted to sell me a flying carpet and when I said that only exists in fairy tales, he put me on it and we took off. I just didn't dare jump down and was forced to sail through the air for two days. But now I'm back. I didn't buy the carpet, it was too delicate for me.

This morning I thought I was in a science fiction movie. All around my house was a transparent wall that I just couldn't get through. Not even the telephone worked. Then in the evening there was a bright flash and the whole spook was over.

A UFO beamed me up and only brought me back to my flat this morning.

There were tomatoes on my plate when I watched the horror film, they've now mutated into killer vegetables, I'll just stay at home until they're all caught.

I'm stuck in a space-time continuum.

The subspace vibrations feel so weird today, I feel really sick.

I couldn't make it. The Borg had assimilated me for two days as a test.

Somehow I felt like Alice in Wonderland: first I'm flung up by a whirlwind, then I arrive somewhere foreign and have the greatest difficulty getting back home. So it's no wonder if you can't be reached for three days.

In reincarnation therapy I learned that in my past life I buried a gold treasure in Alaska. You will understand that I will be out searching for the next few weeks and will not be able to come into the office.

A UFO wanted to blow away the earth because it was in the way of the new intergalactic highway. It took me an enormous amount of time and energy to convince them of a new routing.

King Arthur came to my flat three days ago and said he needed me for the round table. Well, the food and drink was quite nice, but the whole knighthood is a pretty rotten bunch after all.

I dreamt I was the main character in Gulliver's Travels, lying tied up on the beach. The dream was so real that I couldn't move out of bed for several hours.

Despite my protests, the taxi driver drove me to Memphis because he really wanted to show me that Elvis was still alive. But he wasn't at home at the time.

First came this Drought and then the Flood and when the Apocalyptic Horsemen turned the corner, I quickly went home again.

Been out with Batman. At least that's what my perception says. I wonder if I read too many comics over the weekend???

The red of the traffic lights no longer reaches my perception since I have put myself on a higher vibrational level through intensive meditation.

Last night I felt as strong as Arnold in the Terminator, but unfortunately I lost the fight and was still in a coma this morning.

I was abducted by a wild nomadic tribe while on holiday in the Caucasus–now I'm allergic to tents and animal hair.

Someone has hypnotised all the staff and the boss. I only escaped because I was in the toilet.

I couldn't make it earlier, aliens turned my petrol into water.

That had to happen. My karma is so bad today.

Well, I went hiking on Sunday and when I was behind the seven mountains, seven dwarfs came and held me because they thought I was the prince of their Snow White.

Yesterday I caught a virus by e-mail that reset my clock radio, destroyed the chip in the coffee machine, paralysed the remote control for the garage and short-circuited the electrics in my car. Those hackers should really be tarred and feathered!

I'm stuck on a piece of chewing gum right now and can't get loose. Now I'm waiting for the fire service with the Jaws of Life.

My house astrologer says that with my ascendant and Neptune in the 2nd house, there's only trouble.

The cosmic rays are so strong today, they're affecting all the computer parts.

These are the effects of the particle accelerator. Somehow there's too much antimatter in the air here.

Talk to my colleague? Not possible. Scotty has beamed him up.

Once I get through the karma transplant, everything will be better.

Houston had a problem and I had to fix it.